Liza vs. Leukemia

Copyright © 2023 by Liza vs. Leukemia Foundation

All rights reserved.

No portion of this book may be reproduced in any form without written permission from the publisher or author, except as permitted by U.S. copyright law.

Dedicated to:
All the helping hands that came together to meet the needs of Myliza's mind, body, and spirit.

Love comes in many shapes and forms. Never underestimate the power of sharing it with others.

And to all the other warriors facing unimaginable battles.

You are MORE than a conqueror through Him!
His power within you is mightier than any power against you.
Romans 8:37

Hi, my name is Liza Madison.
I'm God's design. His unique creation.
He says I've got power stored deep down in me,
To spread His great goodness for all Earth to see.

Just as heroes wear capes to be set apart.
My cape is a sign that God lives in my heart.

Follow along with me. Soon you will see,
God's power is not only found within me.

Here is my family I'd like you to meet.
They keep my heart light and make life feel complete!

My mom and my dad, guide and defender,
And my big sis, so kind and so tender.

My grandma and grandpa are gifts from above.
They teach me a lot, but the greatest is love.

My life was so happy, with laughter and song,
Until I felt sick—something was wrong!
After two trips to the doctor, concern filled his eyes.
"Stay home and rest," is what he advised.

Being sick and tired just wouldn't subside.
I never felt rested, despite how I tried.
My sickness progressed more and more each day after.
My mind became blurry. There was no more laughter.

Late one night, as Mom tucked me in bed,
Grandma said, "Go to the hospital instead!"

Sitting down at her table and praying in silence,
God leaned in and whispered to her His clear guidance.
"Get Liza to a hospital as fast as you can.
Not to worry, I hold her in the palm of My hands!"

My mom and my dad packed our bags, and we went.
In the hospital waiting room, hours were spent.
We were finally escorted to a room in the back,
Offered a blanket, a drink, and a snack.

The doctor ran tests to look for an answer.
Was it an allergy? Flu? Maybe cancer?
It took a few pokes to draw blood from my vein.
There must be a cause to explain all this pain!

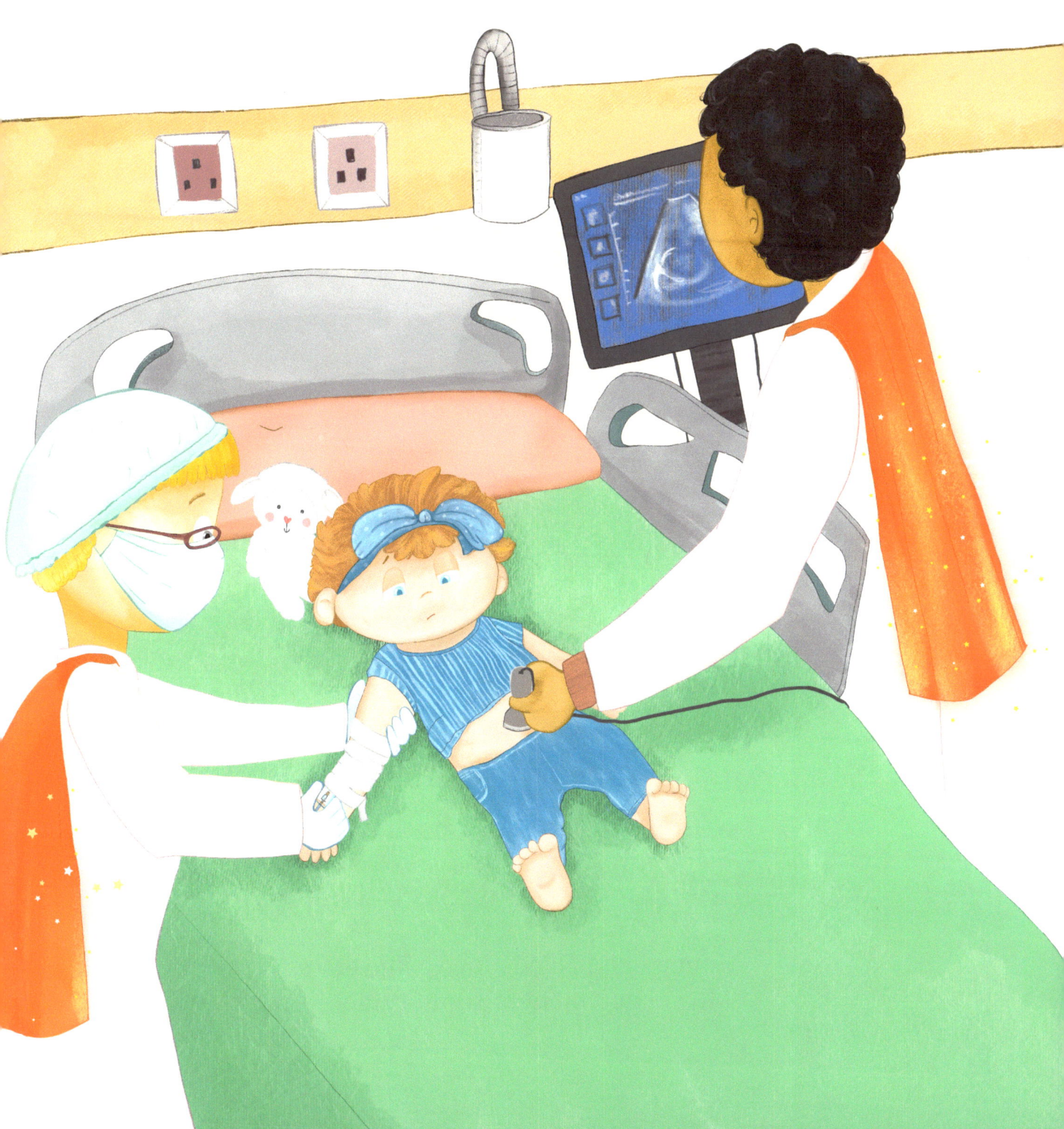

When the doctor was ready and came to the room,
His expression was one filled with anguish and gloom.
With concern, he softly shared the bad news.
Finally, a reason was found for the blues.

Mommy and Daddy broke into tears,
I wanted to hug them to comfort their fears.

I was diagnosed with leukemia that day.
But not to worry, doctor says I'll be okay.
Grandma was using God's power that night.
She walks by her faith and not by her sight.

"What is leukemia?" you might ask the question.
It's a cancer that needs immediate attention.
It may be difficult to understand,
But I will describe it as best as I can.

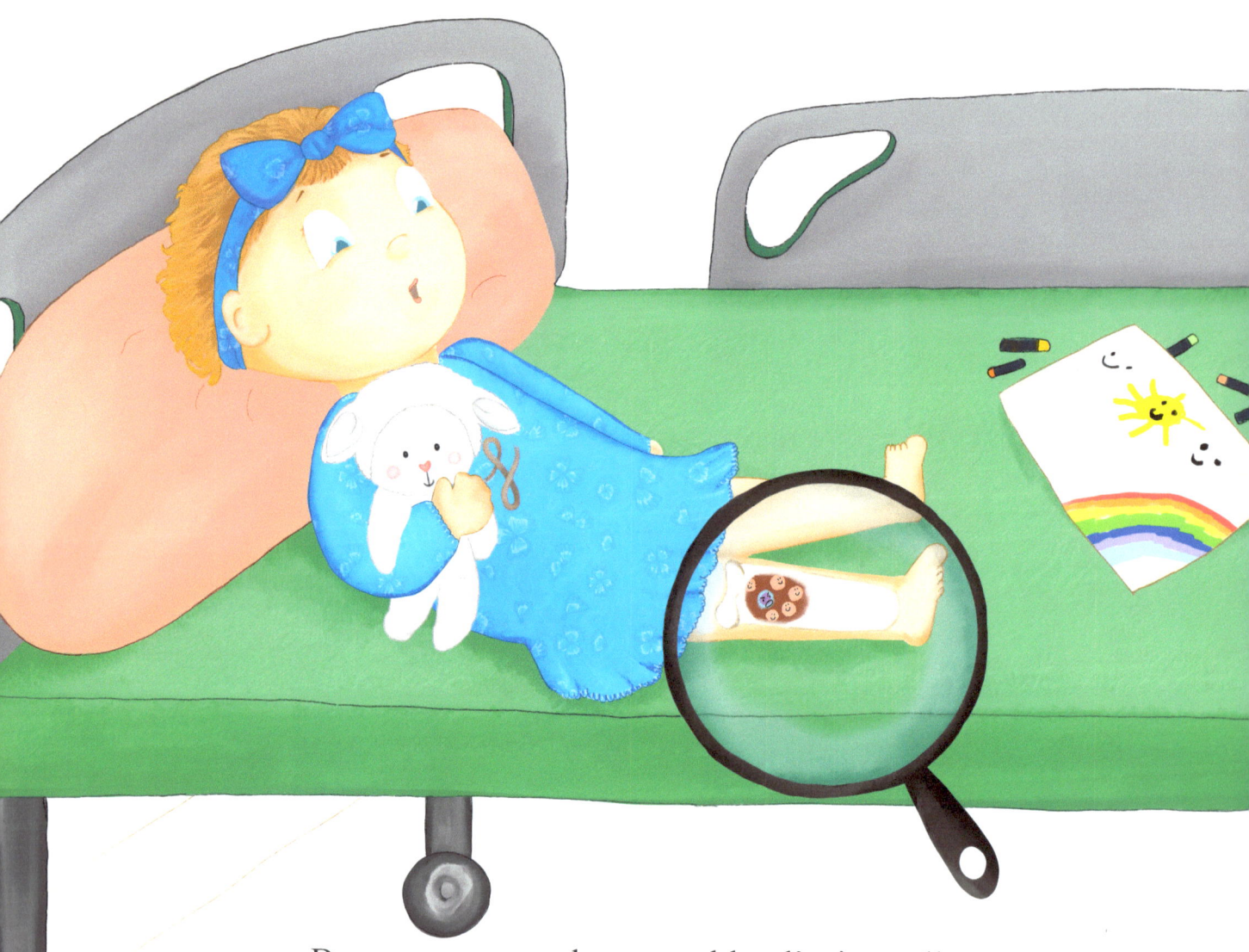

Bone marrow produces our blood's tiny cells,
But, unfortunately for me, just one cell rebelled.
That one bad cell replicated and spread,
And replaced all the healthier blood cells instead.

Chemotherapy was one of the ways,
To make the bad cells in my body obey.
But chemotherapy is not very precise,
And to the good cells, too, it's not very nice.

So, up we went to the very top floor.
These bad cells were something
we couldn't ignore.

I spent lots of time within hospital walls.
I talked with my friends mostly through FaceTime calls.

Each day had its share of darkness and gloom,
It was easy to let the sadness consume.
But God sent reminders that He was quite near.
Through His power He shared through the others so dear.

A few times a day, the nurses would check on me,
And listen a while as I played ukulele.
On bad days, they gave me their love and their grace,
And made the hospital a warm, pleasant place.

They were Heaven's dear angels, it's certainly true.
There was nothing those hospital nurses couldn't do!

Some days were filled with difficult news,
Changing the doctor's medical views.
One day, he said I needed new bone marrow.
"The treatment plan will change tomorrow."

Chemotherapy was not the only way.
New bone marrow was how I'd be okay.

The donor could be my sister, mom, or dad.
They knew it might hurt them but only a tad.
My superhero daddy is whom God chose.
His love for me is selfless, and clearly, it shows.

He donated bone marrow with love from his heart,
And blessed my body with a brand-new start.
My daddy's amazing! Wouldn't you agree?
His God-given power was used on me!

God used real people like you and me.
Formed into heroes to fight the enemy!
Through my story, God's goodness revealed,
In His hands, I'm eternally healed!

Perhaps God is speaking through me to you,
And restoring a hope once within you too!

You are God's design. His unique creation.
Put on your cape and see His transformation!
He says you've got the power inside of you,
And the world will see His goodness through you too!

1 Corinthians 12:4-7 (*New Living Translation*)
"There are different kinds of spiritual gifts [powers], but the same Spirit is the source of them all. There are different kinds of service, but we serve the same Lord. God works in different ways, but it is the same God who does the work in all of us. A spiritual gift [power] is given to each of us so we can help each other."

Reflecting on God's Infinite Power

Many instances of God's infinite power were demonstrated in the story of *Liza vs. Leukemia*. Consider the powers that were used to heal Liza's mind, body, and spirit.

1. <u>Wisdom:</u> The power to recognize and follow God's will in our lives.

2. <u>Knowledge:</u> The power of utilizing biblical scripture to gain understanding of life's challenges.

3. <u>Faith:</u> The power of confidence in God that He will provide, protect, and answer prayers.

4. <u>Healing:</u> The power of prayer, touch, or spoken words to produce spiritual, physical, or emotional healing.

5. <u>Miracles:</u> The power of inviting God into one's life to do extraordinary things.

6. <u>Prophecy:</u> The power of conveying God's message to His people.

7. <u>Discernment:</u> The power of distinguishing between good and evil.

The Power of the C.A.P.E.

Seeking Your God-Given Power

Liza's Grandma invited God into her heart, and by doing so, she opened the door for miracles to take place. Put on your C.A.P.E. and "let God transform you into a new person by changing the way you think. Then you will learn to know God's will for you, which is good and pleasing and perfect" (Romans 12:2 *New Living Translation*).

Try to follow these steps once a day or more to continually welcome God into your life and make way for extraordinary things to happen.

1.) Collect:

Take note of your surroundings and collect information. What do you see, hear, touch, smell, or taste? Try to make three or more observations of what you're experiencing.

2.) Assess:

Assess your current state of mind. How do you feel inside? Look within to try and identify three or more of your emotions.

3.) Pray:

Share your observations and feelings with God. Imagine He is sitting next to you. Every word you speak is valuable to God, our Almighty Creator.

4.) Explore:

How is God communicating with you? God's response is delivered to us in a variety of ways. He might not speak to us with words, but He often places things on our hearts for us to explore.

Ideas derived from
Dr. James G. Johnson: https://drjamesgjohnson.org/

Remember to use "The Power of the C.A.P.E." in all you do, and your Heavenly Father will be so proud of you!

I was born in August, 2021.

At only 4 months old, I began feeling very ill.

God speaks through us when we take the time to listen and respond.

I visited the doctor's office twice, and each time was sent back home with little concern. Soon after, God placed it on my grandma's heart to get me to the hospital as soon as possible.

I was diagnosed with infant leukemia in December, 2021.

Sometimes in between treatment rounds, I would develop a fever that sent me right back to the hospital for intense antibiotic treatment.

Serving dinner shows your support.

My life was flipped upside down! Doctors and nurses worked very hard to help me. I was started on chemotherapy.

In between rounds of chemotherapy I was able to go home. Being home helped refuel my energy to keep fighting the cancer. When I was home, many thoughtful friends brought meals so our family could simply enjoy being together.

Being a visitor brings value to another.

Chemotherapy, unfortunately, has bad side effects like nausea, hair loss, and low energy.

However, it did lift my spirits when visitors came to see me.

In November, 2022 my dad's cells were taken from his body, and transplanted into mine. The cells were ready to attack, but unfortunately began attacking my body too.

Liza's Walk Of Faith
Stumbling Upon God's Power

I developed an inflammatory response called: thrombotic microangiopathy (TMA). This response caused sores in my tummy, and a blockage in my lungs.

Sharing toys brings laughter and joy.

Often, when my dad and sister really missed my mom and me, they would stay nearby at the Ronald McDonald House. They were always provided dinner, and my sister enjoyed playing with all the toys.

Cancer can be very sneaky and find really good hiding spots in my body. One day the doctors found cancer cells hiding in my spine.

Discerning between good and evil can help heal a friend.

This meant we needed to outsmart the cancer, and find stronger ways to attack! The doctors decided to take my T-cells (my fighter cells) and send them to a lab for strengthening. They then were put back into my body to aggressively attack the cancer. This is called CAR-T cell therapy.

Donating blood or bone marrow is a selfless act of love.

While they were attacking the cancer, my body went into a storm! I had a fever, rapid heart rate, and nausea. After the storm subsided I was sent home.

After months of letting the T-cells fight, the doctor said it was now time for a bone marrow transplant. My Dad was the best match for me!

Prayer invites God's presence into the situation.

Would you mind using your God-given power of prayer? Please pray over the cells in my body – that each one obeys. And please pray over my other friends who have rebellious cells too!

At the time of publication I am feeling so happy to be home doing "normal" activities with my family.

After a couple surgical treatments, a dash of steroids, and many prayers I was finally healed and ready to go home!

Liza's Wall of Heroes

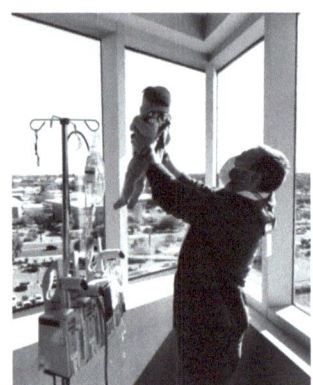

Glenn (Dad) holding Myliza in the "quiet lounge" at Banner Desert Medical Center in Mesa, AZ weeks after the initial diagnosis.

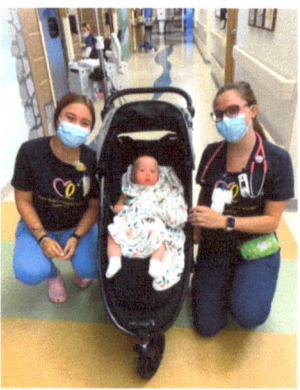

Jordan (patient care technician) and Helen (nurse) posing with Myliza in the hallway during a stroll.

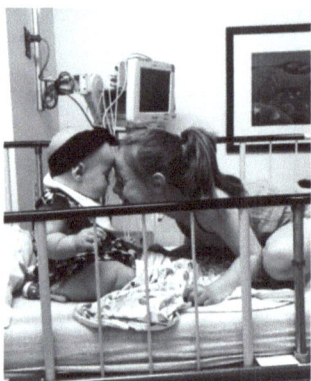

Myliza with M'Rylee (sister) during an outpatient chemotherapy session early on in treatment.

Janette (Charity's friend) and Josie (Myliza's bestie) celebrating their 1/2 birthdays together at Banner Desert Medical Center.

M'Rylee celebrating with Myliza that she is 100% cancer free after induction chemotherapy treatment. Sign placed by the Maricopa Running Club.

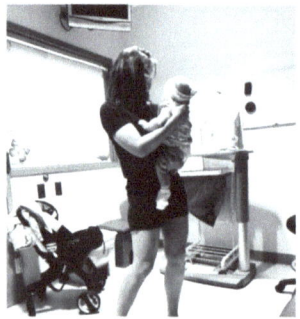

Charity (mom) holding Myliza post central line placement operation.

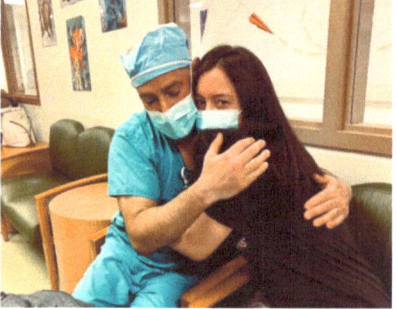

Dr. Greenfeld (pediatric surgeon) providing comfort to Charity post central line placement operation.

Chad (uncle) posing for a photo with Myliza post central line placement.

Cherrye (family friend) holding Myliza during a day of inpatient chemotherapy.

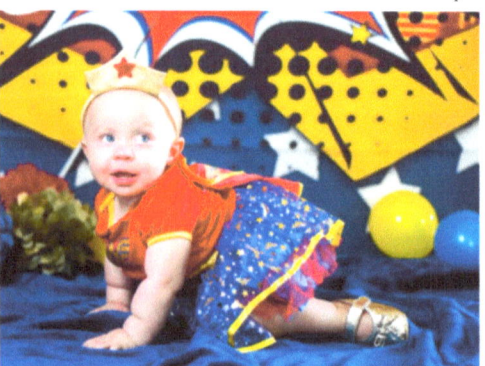

MyLiza representing ONE-der woman as she celebrates her first birthday with friends and family.

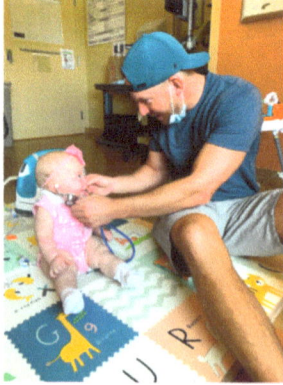

Ricky (uncle) playing doctor with Myliza during her visit at Banner University Medical Center in Tucson, AZ for Car-T cell therapy.

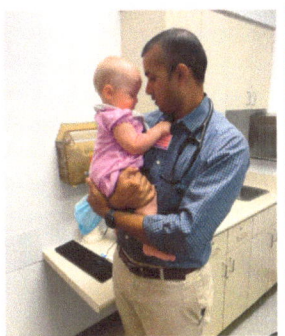
Dr. Reddivalla (pediatric oncologist) comforting MyLiza during a weekly clinic visit prior to bone marrow transplant (BMT).

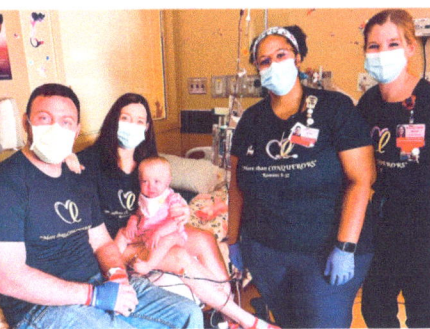
Glenn, Charity, Myliza, Kindra (nurse), and Kayla (nurse) minutes prior to the BMT.

Glenn laying with Myliza during BMT procedure.

Glenn, M'Rylee, Myliza, and Charity celebrating Christmas as a family at Banner University Medical Center.

Myliza reading over the prayers that were sent to her from a women's bible study group at La Plata Valley Baptist Church.

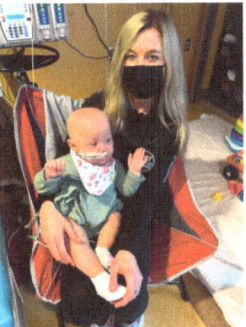
Brittney (aunt) comforting Myliza prior to her transfer to the PICU post-BMT.

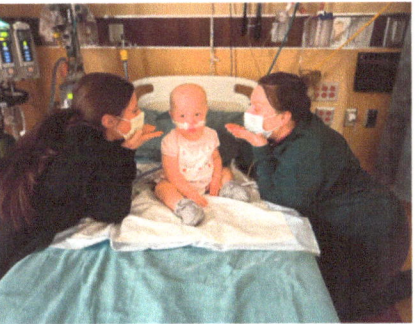
Rachel (nurse) and Megan (nurse) checking in on Myliza during her brief stay in the PICU post-transplant.

Ronda (grandma) and Rick (grandpa) celebrating Myliza's brief moment outside of the Banner University Medical Center with whipped cream and fruit.

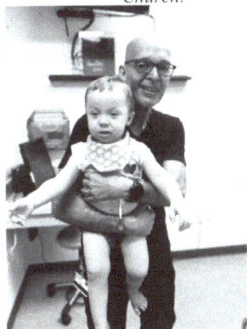
Dr. Katsanis (BMT doctor) holding Myliza at her 8-month post-BMT milestone appointment.

Veronica (great aunt) reading a book with Myliza at an outpatient clinic visit.

Myliza and Erin (childlife specialist) happy to be reunited after Liza's treacherous transplant journey.

M'Rylee holding Myliza as they celebrate 100-day post-BMT milestone at Church of Celebration in Maricopa, AZ.

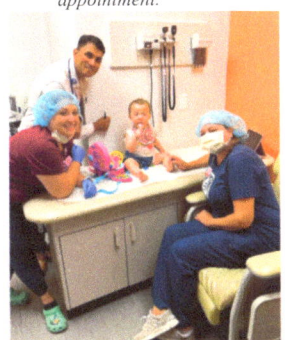
Hannah (nurse), Dr. Reddivalla, and Andrea (nurse) celebrating Myliza's final central line dressing change.

Left to Right: Richard, M'Rylee, Glenn holding Myliza, Charity and Ronda

Glossary

Bone marrow: The spongy substance located in the center of a bone.

Bone marrow transplant: The movement of stem cells from one person to another.

Cancer: a disease that involves the spreading of abnormal cells.

Cell: The basic building block of all living things.

Chemotherapy: A treatment of disease by the use of chemical substances.

Donor: A person who provides blood, organ, or tissue for transplantation.

Leukemia: A disease in which the bone marrow and other blood-forming organs produce an increased number of abnormal leukocytes. The disease is represented by an orange ribbon.

About the Author

Charity Madison obtained her master's degree in counseling from Colorado Christian University, igniting her passion to walk alongside others as they discover their identity in Christ. She is wed to Glenn, and together they share two beautiful daughters. Unfortunately, at only 4 months old, their youngest daughter was diagnosed with an aggressive form of infant leukemia. Her cancer diagnosis was just the beginning of a lengthy treatment journey that encountered many unexpected twists and turns. Despite the many challenges, Myliza's family experienced the presence of God through the spiritual gifts shared by others. The healing of Myliza's mind, body, and spirit was accomplished through the collaboration of all the hands involved in her care. Charity was prompted to share Liza's story to convey a message of hope to children around the world who are fighting unimaginable battles.

About the Illustrator

Steffi Andrat Faria is wife to Edgar, mother to two energetic boys and loves to draw! She was raised in India where she studied medicine and is an MD in Physical Medicine and Rehabilitation. Currently she's staying home with her boys.

As a child, she was drawn to picture books. When she started illustrating, she captured Bible verses in pictures and called them "Scripture Pictures". Slowly, she ventured into illustrating children's books and she has never had so much fun!

Find her on Instagram @scripture.pictures.316

www.ingramcontent.com/pod-product-compliance
Lightning Source LLC
LaVergne TN
LVHW072056070426
835508LV00002B/128